Original title:
Gassy Giants and Giggles

Copyright © 2025 Creative Arts Management OÜ
All rights reserved.

Author: Victor Mercer
ISBN HARDBACK: 978-1-80567-799-4
ISBN PAPERBACK: 978-1-80567-920-2

Jovial Journeys of the Skyfolk

With fluffy clouds as boats they sail,
Their laughter echoes like a tale.
They dance on breezes, oh so spry,
While munching on a pie in the sky.

The sun is winking, stars lay low,
Puffing cheeks in a jovial show.
Each twist and turn gives rise to cheer,
As rainbows sprout from every rear.

Hiccups in the Stratosphere

Up above where the wild winds play,
A hiccup sends the clouds astray.
Each puffy burst a giggling sound,
As giggles ripple all around.

The moonlit glows, a starlit prance,
As comets join in the silly dance.
With every hiccup, laughter flies,
Creating ripples in the skies.

Whimsical Windswept Wonders

A windy wiggle, a frolicsome flit,
As clouds play tag, they barely sit.
With playful nudges and cheeky blows,
They tease the sun and tickle the crows.

In cotton candy skies so bright,
Wonders whirl in pure delight.
Their fun-filled frolic soft and round,
Brings smiles to all who dance around.

Tumult of Tittering Titans

Titans tumble in playful glee,
With thunderous chuckles, wild and free.
They leap and bound with joyful fright,
Creating storms of pure delight.

Each rumbling laugh shakes the trees,
As they share tales that make one sneeze.
Their silly squabbles fill the air,
With joyous echoes everywhere.

Cosmic Comedies Unfold

In the void where planets play,
Stars burst forth in bright ballet.
Laughter echoes through the night,
As comets twirl in pure delight.

Asteroids bounce with glee and cheer,
While moons erupt in jovial sphere.
Galactic jesters prance around,
In the cosmos, joy is found.

Whirlwinds of Whimsy

Twisting, turning through the sky,
A gust of fun that swirls on by.
Clouds are ticklish, watch them soar,
With playful puffs, they'll ask for more.

Blowing hats and ruffling hair,
Mischief waits upon the air.
Laughing breezes rush and chase,
In this wild, enchanting place.

Softly Blowing Mischief

A gentle tickle on the cheek,
With breezy quirks it starts to speak.
The sun winks down with a grin,
As blitheful whispers swirl within.

Ballooning colors fill the street,
With playful leaps and dancing feet.
Every gust a funny jest,
In this mirthful, breezy fest.

Airy Antics Above

Kites at play in azure heights,
Soaring free, oh what a sight!
With giggles caught in every breeze,
They swoop and dip with graceful ease.

Puffy shapes parade and prance,
In their bright and fluffy dance.
Above the world, they spin and sway,
As laughter glides on winds that play.

Grins of the Great Ones

In a land of giants tall and wide,
They chuckle and puff with every stride.
Their laughter rumbles, shakes the ground,
While silly screams of jest abound.

With every step, a thunderous cheer,
Bristling clouds take off in fear.
They valve their jokes, full of glee,
And all of nature laughs in spree.

Clouds with a Sense of Humor

Fluffy fluffies in the sky,
Wobble, wobble, as they fly.
Kidding one another, tossing shade,
Chortling softly, green with trade.

They drop their raindrops, dance around,
Each little splash causes a sound.
With giggles that echo through the air,
These merry clouds have not a care.

Skyward Snores

Beneath the stars, the titans lay,
With snores that rumble night and day.
Their belly laughs make ripples wide,
Waking critters who seek to hide.

With a rumble and shake, the bushes sway,
As humor floats on the milky way.
Sleepy giants enjoying their dreams,
Snoring sounds like bubbling streams.

Celestial Laughter Symphony

A concert high, the heavens sing,
With giggles soft, and wild spring.
All the stars in bright array,
Twinkle winks as shadows play.

The planets jive, a jolly show,
Comets giggle as they fly low.
A chorus loud, a whimsical tune,
Echoes softly beneath the moon.

Breezy Behemoths

In the sky, they float and play,
With a whoosh that brightens the day.
Belly laughs and clouds that sway,
Their soft whispers chase cares away.

A rumble here, a chuckle there,
Puffy bodies with whimsical flair.
They tickle the sun with playful air,
As silly songs fill the atmosphere.

With every bounce, a giggling sound,
Bubbles of joy twist all around.
In their dance, laughter is found,
As fluffy laughter knows no bound.

Oh, see them frolic, wide and free,
Giant pals in harmony.
Their breath is a breeze, a funny spree,
Playing tricks like giddy glee.

Chuckles in the Sky

Fluffy forms in a grand parade,
They wiggle and jiggle, unafraid.
Laughter floats, a blissful serenade,
As they dance on the clouds they've made.

Watch them tumble with silly flair,
Turbulent warmth fills the fresh air.
Rolling giggles from everywhere,
Their jovial tricks, beyond compare.

With a puff, a burst of delight,
Creating rainbows, sparkling bright.
They whisper secrets on a moonlit flight,
Turning worries to sheer light.

Laughter echoes from heights so grand,
A chorus led by a jovial band.
In the skies, let joy be planned,
For every giggle, they've got a hand.

Sighs of Celestial Titans

Titans of wonder fill the skies,
Breaths of humor in mighty guise.
A sigh here, a chuckle that flies,
As twilight dances, time complies.

Playful shadows stretching wide,
With every puff, joy takes a ride.
Up above where raucous chides,
Each wave of laughter softly glides.

They swirl and twirl, a tender tease,
Gales that tickle like a warm breeze.
Their whispers float with effortless ease,
To spin the heart, to bend the knees.

When spirits lift and hearts delight,
They paint the world in hues of bright.
Heaven's jesters, a wondrous sight,
With every laugh, they take to flight.

Echoes of Enchanted Breath

In twilight's glow, they start to play,
Huffing puffs in a merry ballet.
With each exhale, they steal away,
The cares of the world, they sway and sway.

Crescent smiles across the sky,
With wisps of laughter whirling high.
Every whisper a gleeful sigh,
Tracing dreams as they drift by.

Like balloons that dared to roam,
They fill the air, far from home.
Every giggle a frothy poem,
In the skies, they joyfully comb.

Together they frolic, oh so grand,
In a realm where all's unplanned.
With echoes of mirth that brightly stand,
Each enchanted breath, a playful hand.

Skyward Frolics

In the sky, a rumble and roar,
Laughter floats, they want more.
Bubbles dance in a crazy race,
Clouds giggle, oh what a place!

Fluffy forms that twist and play,
Swaying gently, come what may.
Puffs of joy in a bright blue sea,
Nature's jesters, wild and free.

Every gust brings a chuckling breeze,
Wiggling wisps among the trees.
They frolic high, leap and soar,
Tickling fancies, we can't ignore.

So look up high, and you might see,
A world of mirth, pure jubilee.
Let your worries float away,
Join the fun of this airy play.

The Amusement of Airy Whirlwinds

Whirlwinds swirl with playful delight,
Twirling leaves in a whimsical flight.
Chasing shadows, they skip and spin,
Laughter echoed, soft and thin.

Giggles rise in the gentle draft,
Clouds roll over, a frothy craft.
Breezes ripple, a cheerful sound,
Floating joys all around.

Round and round, they twist and tease,
Swaying branches, tickling knees.
Whispers of chuckles ride the air,
Every moment, without a care.

So feel the pulse of the breezy fun,
Where warmth and glee always run.
Lift your head, let your heart align,
With the playfulness of the divine.

Billowing Bliss and Chuckles

Puffy treasures drift and sway,
Twinkling stars in a joyful display.
Giggles bounce on a breezy sigh,
As zany clouds go dancing by.

The sunlight joins with a glimmer bright,
Waves of laughter, a pure delight.
Hovering high, they swirl and glide,
In this whimsical, airy tide.

Each little puff, a tale to tell,
As they tumble, and laugh so well.
Softly musing in the blue,
Sharing secrets just for you.

Laughter blooms in the softest hue,
As the whispers swirl like morning dew.
Join the fun soaring so high,
In this billowing joy, up to the sky.

Jovial Whispers in the Ether

In the ether, whispers gleam,
Joyful tales like a silly dream.
Puffs of mirth that spin around,
Giggles echo, a playful sound.

Little clouds with frothy grins,
Twisting as they leap and spin.
Playful breezes dance with flair,
Tickling laughter fills the air.

Every gust, a chance to play,
Wishes carried far away.
In this laughter, bright and light,
Hearts are lifted to great height.

So close your eyes and take a breath,
Find the fun, feel the zest.
For in the whispers, joy awaits,
A merriment that captivates.

Comic Cloudscapes

Above the fields, so fluffy and bright,
Laughter echoes in the warm sunlight.
Puffy creatures bounce in playful cheer,
Tickling the air, spreading joy far and near.

Wobbling wonders drift on a breeze,
Chasing each other with giggles and wheezes.
They twist and tumble, burst into mirth,
Creating a circus high above the earth.

Chunky forms roll in a silly parade,
Mischievous shapes on their journey laid.
Bubbles of jest float on all around,
As colorful giggles swirl through the sound.

In this realm where joy takes flight,
Clouds play tricks until the night.
With laughter brightening the endless skies,
It's a show of whimsy that never says goodbye.

Floating Frolics in the Firmament

Up in the blue, where the fluffy roam,
Whirls of delight, far from home.
They dive and dash, and do pirouettes,
Spreading pure smiles, no regrets.

Bouncing through rays of the sun's warm glow,
Silly figures in an aerial show.
They puff and they blow, making it rain,
With sprinkle of giggles, they dance through the pain.

Frothy frolics above the trees,
Twisting and turning, just like a breeze.
Bouncing and bubbling, they scatter our fears,
Filling the air with soft, silly cheers.

In the vastness, where the oddities bloom,
Each frolicsome puff dispels the gloom.
With a wink and a laugh, they float far and wide,
In their merry escapade, joy won't hide.

Unseen Wonders and Soft Chuckles

In the sky where no one peeks,
Bubbles form with laughter's squeaks.
Dancing in a breezy fun,
Tickled by the morning sun.

Floating friends in hues so bright,
Spreading joy, what a sight!
Whispers swirl on gentle breeze,
Bringing smiles with greatest ease.

Spirited Airship Antics

Up above in a jolly float,
A merry band in a silly boat.
Chasing dreams on cotton trails,
Sailing far where laughter sails.

The captain roars while sailors grin,
With every twist, the fun begins.
Puffing air in cheeky glee,
Unruly joy is wild and free.

Whispers of Whimsical Winds

Gentle breezes tell a tale,
As fluffy shapes begin to sail.
With every gust, a chuckle too,
A joyous dance, a twenty-two.

Tickling noses, teasing hair,
Up they go without a care.
In this world, where grins abound,
Laughter echoes all around.

Laughter among the Clouds

Above the world, where fluffy roam,
   Giggling clouds find their home.
  A burst of joy in every puff,
  Creating fun that's never tough.

Skies are filled with jolly tunes,
Soft shouts from bouncing buffoons.
  Every wink that colors the blue,
   Brings delighted hearts anew.

Whimsy Amongst the Cloud Castles

Up above the land, they play,
Chasing fluffy dreams away,
With every bounce and wobbly twist,
They giggle loud in misty bliss.

Round and round they swirl and spin,
Tumbling softly on a whim,
A twinkle here, a sparkle there,
Cloudy capers fill the air.

With a puff, they float and sway,
Tickling breezes in their play,
Mirthful shadows dance below,
As laughter sings in joyful flow.

In vibrant hues, they paint the sky,
With chuckles echoing on high,
As everyone looks on in glee,
Join the fun, the world must see!

Laughter Wrapped in Mist

In a swirl of dreams so bright,
They twirl and twist, a silly sight,
With every giggle that they share,
Magic bubbles fill the air.

Puffy cheeks and sparkly eyes,
Floating gently through the skies,
Giggling sprites in playful flight,
Wrapped in whispers of delight.

With a whoosh, an airy cheer,
They turn the clouds to joyful spheres,
Bouncing lightly, full of cheer,
With fits of laughter ringing clear.

Down below, the earthlings grin,
As they watch the antics spin,
With every puff and soft parade,
The misty mirth will never fade.

Roars of Delight on High

Beneath the sun and azure blue,
A chorus of chuckles, bright and true,
Echoing laughter from the skies,
Where every wisp is a sweet surprise.

Fluffy whispers twist and glide,
Silly antics cannot hide,
Each balloon that floats away,
Sparks more giggles as they play.

Up above the realm of dreams,
Bashing clouds with playful beams,
Up and down, they swirl with glee,
As laughter booms like a symphony.

In the heights, where joy takes wing,
Every puff and roar can sing,
It's a festival, wild and free,
Where the hearty laughter floats like sea.

The Humorous Haze

In the misty veil of the morn,
A band of pranksters was reborn,
Bubbling giggles, swirling bright,
With every turn, they take to flight.

Chasing shadows, hiding snug,
With whispers soft, a playful tug,
In that haze of chuckles loud,
Their silly games tickle the crowd.

Bouncers bouncing, giggling away,
Floating softly on a sunny day,
With hearty howls and silly fits,
Creating joy with quirky bits.

Through the haze, they prance and sway,
Painting smiles in every way,
The world beneath begins to cheer,
For laughter reigns, forever near.

Dance of the Drifting Clouds

In the sky, balloons sway,
Big puffs play hide and seek.
They twirl and swirl all day,
With soft giggles that peek.

A fuzzy friend floats high,
Making silly shapes and forms.
With a chuckle in the sky,
He weathers all the storms.

Bouncing off a sunbeam's glow,
A parade of laughs unite.
Up in the air, we go,
In a feather-like delight.

Joyously they sail fast,
Causing chuckles all around.
In a whimsical blast,
Laughter's where they're found.

Amusement in the Atmosphere

Up above, the laughter rings,
As fluffy clouds have fun.
They play with shadowy swings,
Beneath the shining sun.

A comet whizzes by, oh my!
With a giggle, what a sight!
The stars all wink as they fly,
In the cover of the night.

Wobbly shapes twist and bend,
As they dance without a care.
Every twist a joke, my friend,
Float on pockets of the air.

Every breeze brings silly cheer,
Filling hearts with carefree glee.
Floating far, we disappear,
In joyful mystery.

Rolling Laughter in the Stratosphere

Whirling up in sky so vast,
Round and round the breezes twirl.
With each whoosh, a good time cast,
As fluffy puffs do swirl.

They tumble, frolic, spin and play,
Like mischievous little sprites.
In the air, they find their way,
Causing giggles, pure delights.

Bright rainbows form in their wake,
A cartoon dance of color and sound.
Through the skies, the chuckles quake,
As giggling echoes bounce around.

High above, joy takes its flight,
In a feathery, joyous spree.
Rolling laughter day and night,
As we all float wild and free.

Rising Roars of Delight

Up they go, a fluffy bike,
Riding on the wind with ease.
Clouds with smiles, ready to strike,
With giggles drifting in the breeze.

They paint the sky with bright ideas,
Every puff a playful jest.
Echoing through the atmosphere,
Their laughter blooms, never guessed.

Bouncing thoughts and sparkly dreams,
Together in a sky-high play.
With every sparkle, laughter beams,
A chorus of joy on display.

Floating on their puffy thrills,
Creating fun with every twist.
In the air, where laughter spills,
They dance, the clouds, in bliss.

Bewitched by Ballooning Bliss

A jolly round shape floats high,
With colors bright against the sky.
Bouncing like a feathered fool,
Making each kid feel like a jewel.

The wind blows strong, it laughs and sings,
It's deftly plucking all our strings.
A whimsical dance, a merry flight,
Chasing clouds throughout the night.

Laughter erupts with every rise,
As shadows play and spark the skies.
We're twirling with joy, light as air,
Each bubble bursting with playful flair.

Floating away, our worries cease,
In this frolic, we find our peace.
With hearts of cheer, we take our chance,
In ballooning bliss, we laugh and dance.

Updrafts of Uproar

Whirlwinds bring a ticklish tease,
As swirls of giggles dance with ease.
Crisp breezes pop like bubbling beer,
Each gust a shout, a playful cheer.

Clouds are fluffy, in funny shapes,
Like silly hats on grinning apes.
With every puff, they twist and squeak,
A jocular world, far from bleak.

A chorus of chuckles fills the air,
As all our worries seem so rare.
Updrafts whisper, "Come play along,"
In this rollicking form of song!

In this ruckus, we find our way,
Through waves of laughter, we sway and play.
So, let's lift off and join the ruck,
With updrafts of uproar, we will erupt!

Ethereal Eruptions of Ecstasy

From deep within the azure dome,
Bubbles burst, they find their home.
A giggly puff, a squeaky boom,
Riding the waves, we laugh and zoom.

Popping sounds like candy rain,
Each eruption drives away pain.
In this dance of joy and cheer,
We spin and twirl, there's nothing to fear!

A comet's trail of sparkling fun,
Laughing sunbeams, we can't outrun.
Each twinkle in our eyes reflects,
The sass of chaos it collects.

So, come and join this hearty spree,
As giggles stir the wild, free sea.
With every chuckle, we're set to soar,
In ethereal eruptions, forevermore!

Spirited Spirals in the Sky

Spinning high on breezy curls,
Polliwogs twist and playful swirls.
Every laugh a rocket flare,
As we ride the spiral air.

Up we fly with squeals of glee,
In a tangle of merry spree.
With glimmers bright and chatter loud,
We become the frolicking crowd.

Whirling round, we take our chance,
In spirals of joy, we gleefully prance.
With each twist, the giggles grow,
In this spirited flight, we let them flow.

So grab a hand, let's reach new heights,
In the spiral dance of dazzling lights.
Together we'll jest, and from the sky,
We'll hang on tightly, and never say die!

Rushing Currents of Comedic Relief

In the river where laughter flows,
Silly fish dance on their toes.
Bubbles pop with a loud delight,
Splashing joy in the warm sunlight.

Jokes leap out like frogs in spring,
Tickling the air, oh what they bring!
A current of chuckles swirls around,
Making amusing waves with each sound.

Witty reeds whisper in the breeze,
Telling tales that tickle with ease.
The water winks as it giggles bright,
Gifting a chuckle to day and night.

So, glide on, dear friends, on this stream,
Where humor swells and dreams redeem.
Let the current carry your frowns away,
In this flood of laughter, forever stay.

Skyward Symphony of Sighs

Up in the clouds where the giggles soar,
Funny sounds drift and often explore.
A symphony made of whimsical tones,
Tickling the hearts of the giggling drones.

Puffy creatures float with delight,
Tickling the stars in the soft moonlight.
A trumpet made from a laughing breeze,
Making melodies that dance with ease.

As moonbeams dance to the jester's tune,
Life's little quirks make us swoon.
Silly shadows leap and prance,
In this light-hearted, nighttime dance.

So join in the fun, let your spirits fly,
Lift off from the ground, we'll touch the sky.
In this whimsical world where joy never dies,
Breathe deep the laughter, in skyward sighs.

Hilarity in the High Skies

Up above where the eagles nest,
Giggles erupt from the very best.
The wind tickles high, a playful tease,
While clouds tumble down with the greatest of ease.

Kites dance wildly on invisible strings,
Flapping and flailing, just like living things.
Balloons drift past, they squeal with delight,
Wobbling and wobbling in the bright twilight.

Airships full of laughter puff along,
Horns honking playfully, joining the song.
A parade of giggles floats by with flair,
Bringing smiles to every face in the air.

So let your heart soar, let humor ignite,
Join in the fun from morning till night.
In the high skies, where the joy multiplies,
Follow the laughter, and let spirits rise.

Blustering Beasties of the Breeze

Windswept creatures of funny design,
Roar with laughter, oh how they shine.
With fluffy tails and grins so wide,
They scatter joy with the changing tide.

Breezy beasts with a sassy prance,
Twirl and whirl, throwing a dance.
Riding the gusts, they tumble and roll,
In a whimsically funny, frolicsome stroll.

Jokes on the air, tickling each tree,
As the leaves giggle and join in glee.
Blustering laughs that fill up the space,
Creating a symphony, a whimsical race.

So hear their chuckles, oh so bold,
Join on this ride, let the stories unfold.
With every gust, let laughter increase,
As the breezes deliver their comical peace.

Ballooned Jests of the Cosmos

In the sky, odd forms do play,
Round and bouncy, they sway all day.
Stars chuckle down at their fun-filled dance,
Floating softly, in a whimsical trance.

With puffs of air, they twist and twirl,
Chasing each other in a giggling swirl.
Their silly faces puffed with glee,
Echoing laughter across the sea.

Laughter from the Atmosphere

Above the clouds, a wild parade,
Bubbles of joy that never fade.
Whispers of delight in the winds do cheer,
Each whoosh and woosh brings the world near.

A tickle of air, a playful breeze,
Spreads giggles and chuckles through the trees.
Feathers and clouds, a delightful mix,
Creating a ruckus with a few funny tricks.

Enigmatic Breezes and Joyful Roars

Curly wisps that tease and spin,
Carrying laughter from within.
Not a soul can help but grin,
As whoopee cushions echo the din.

With mighty gusts, a game unfolds,
Tales of muffled laughter told.
Each roar of wind, a joyful jest,
Making the daytime feel like a fest.

Raucous Revelries Above

In twilight's glow, balloons take flight,
Each one wobbling in pure delight.
Chasing rainbows, they giggle and bounce,
In a wondrous wheel where laughter's pronounced.

Stars join in with twinkles bright,
Winking down on this merry sight.
A swirling waltz of silly sounds,
Filling the air with joy that astounds.

Festive Frights

In the night, shadows dance,
With a howl, they take a chance.
Pumpkins grin, eyes aglow,
Boisterous chuckles start to flow.

Broomsticks zoom in the air,
Ghosts giggle without a care.
Monsters pulling funny faces,
Joy erupts in wild embraces.

Chasing bats with silly hats,
Mischief made by playful gnats.
The eerie sound of honks and squeaks,
In this spooky world, laughter peaks.

A haunted house filled with cheer,
Echoes of laughter we all hear.
From shadows, the spirits peek,
With every scare, we all just squeak.

Raindrop Revels

Pitter-patter on the ground,
Jumping puddles all around.
Wiggly worms jump with glee,
In the rain, we're wild and free.

Dancing drops with merry slaps,
Splashing knees and gentle taps.
Umbrellas upside-down and high,
With a wink, the clouds go by.

Rubber ducks float with delight,
Bubble chatter fills the night.
Rainboots stomp like happy clowns,
Waves of joy that can't come down.

Silly hats and raincoats bright,
Every heart feels pure delight.
Raindrops fall but smiles stay,
Together we laugh all day.

Chaotic Chortles from the Cosmos

Stars wobble in the midnight sky,
While comets zoom with a cheerful sigh.
Galaxies twirl in spiraling spins,
And the universe chuckles with wins.

Aliens dance on Saturn's rings,
Inventing all sorts of funny things.
They trade jokes with planetary friends,
As laughter echoes, never ends.

Shooting stars throw witty quips,
Tickling moons and solar flips.
Asteroids bounce with glee and pride,
In this cosmic joke, we all reside.

Whimsical orbs in vibrant hues,
Spin tales that tickle and amuse.
In the depths of space so vast,
Laughter spreads, forever cast.

Lively Laughter in Latitudes

On sunny shores where seagulls play,
The surf sings tunes in a merry way.
Sandcastles made with giggling hands,
As footprints dance across the sands.

In mountain peaks where breezes rise,
Echoing joy beneath blue skies.
Silly yodels from the heights,
Break the calm, ignite delights.

Forest trails alive with cheer,
Every rustle brings us near.
Squirrels chase in playful strife,
Bringing smiles to all our life.

While city streets buzz with a laugh,
As strangers share a witty gaffe.
In this world of fun and glee,
Laughter bonds both you and me.

Airy Whimsy and Winks

In a field where laughter roams,
Breezes dance like playful gnomes.
They swirl and sway, a funny tune,
Under the watch of a giggling moon.

Tickles in the air are found,
As silly sounds spin all around.
Winks exchanged with every puff,
Creating joy, just light and and gruff.

With each gust, the flowers sway,
Waving hello to the silly play.
Laughter spills from every leaf,
Making moments feel like a brief.

So let the air play its tricks,
In the light of the moon, it flows and flicks.
An airy whimsy, a funny sight,
Bringing smiles through the night.

Breezy Buddies Beneath the Stars

Under the vast and sparkling sky,
Breezy friends let out a sigh.
With every puff, the clouds react,
Sending giggles in a playful pact.

Each figment whispers a warm jest,
As breezes tumble, they find their zest.
Rolling laughter, a comet's tail,
Filling the night with a light veil.

Frolicking whispers, stories unfold,
Tales of the bold, the bright, the old.
In the cool night, mischief awakes,
Shared among friends, as laughter quakes.

So gather 'round, both near and far,
Breath light and bold as you gaze at a star.
Under this blanket, we all combine,
In breezy camaraderie, we brightly shine.

Elysian Escapades of the Air

Where the clouds prance and play all day,
In the open skies, we find our way.
A burst of laughter, a joyful sigh,
In every moment, we float on high.

Whispers of joy fill the azure sea,
Every giggle, an ode to glee.
With each swirl, the air takes flight,
Like little sprites in the heart of night.

Mischief is brewing, oh what a sight,
As we frolic and spin in pure delight.
Elysian bounds, we jump and cheer,
Hopping through clouds, without a fear.

Dancing in rhythm with breezy tunes,
While laughter echoes, beneath the moons.
In joyous dances, we lose each care,
Celebrating life in the light and air.

Tantalizing Toots of Fun

In the realm where chuckles soar,
Silly sounds bring joy to the core.
With every puff, a giggle breaks,
And laughter ripples in funny wakes.

The air is filled with playful blows,
Creating giggles as each one flows.
A bubbling brook of jibes and jests,
As friends unite in the silliness.

Each sound a song of merry delight,
Through the air, it dances, takes flight.
With every twist and playful tease,
We drift along with joyful ease.

So raise a cheer to the funny breeze,
In swooshing gusts, it aims to please.
With every laugh, we come undone,
In the parade of tantalizing fun.

Sassy Sky Dancers

In the sky, there swirls a flight,
With colors bold, oh, what a sight!
They twist and twirl in playful glee,
Sprinkling joy for all to see.

A wobbly dance, a silly leap,
Floating high, no time for sleep.
With breezy laughs, they frolic free,
Like kites that laugh in harmony.

They trade some jests with clouds above,
And all the stars, they wink in love.
A giggle here, a snicker there,
Their laughter fills the frosty air.

So join the fun, take to the sky,
With sassy moves, we'll dance and fly!
In every twirl, let giggles reign,
In this grand show, there's no more pain.

Breezy Banter in the Ether

Whispers swirl on zephyr's wings,
Bathed in light, the laughter rings.
A jolly crew of puffs and pings,
Race through clouds, oh, what joy it brings!

With every gust, a chuckle flows,
In playful games, the wind bestows.
They trade their tales, both bright and cheeky,
Creating mirth so warm and sneaky.

From sunlit beams to shadowy nooks,
Join in the fun, let's write the books!
With breezy jests and witty rhymes,
We dance through air in merry times.

So lift your spirits, come take a ride,
In the lovely laugh-filled tide.
For where the winds of joy do blow,
We find the light in every show.

Curlicues of Cosmic Joy

In the cosmos, there twists a grin,
With spiraled shapes, let fun begin.
A twinkling star gives out a cheer,
As curlicues of joy appear.

They bounce and roll through space so wide,
With sparkles that the comets ride.
Giggles burst from planets' play,
As laughter lights the Milky Way.

A dance of bubbles, whispers soar,
With every twist, a laugh galore.
In cosmic realms, where wonders frolic,
The funny vibes are truly iconic.

So join the dance, embrace the spin,
With cheeky smiles, let the fun in!
In this vast space where joy's the key,
Let curlicues of laughter be!

Laughter on the Currents

Across the waves, a cheerful rip,
Where laughter bubbles, takes a trip.
The ocean sings in chuckles bright,
As currents flow with pure delight.

Fishy friends with silly ways,
Join in the frolic, sparkly sprays.
They leap and dive, a splashy game,
In the water, joy's the name!

With swirling tides and playful swells,
The sea reveals its funny tales.
From dolphins' flips to seaweed's sway,
Laughter carries on the waves today.

So listen close, let giggles guide,
On water's crest, we come alive.
For with each ripple, joy's affirmed,
In laughter's dance, our hearts are warmed.

Jovial Giants at Play

In the land where laughter roams,
The giants dance on fluffy foams.
With silly hats and shoes so bright,
They twirl and spin, what a delight!

With thunderous laughs that shake the air,
Each giant's joke a playful dare.
They tumble, roll, and bump with glee,
Creating giggles, can't you see?

A game of tag on clouds above,
Chasing rainbows, spreading love.
Their chuckles echo through the sky,
As puffy clouds drift by and sigh.

When twilight falls, they gather round,
With tales of fun, their joy profound.
In this realm where mirth holds sway,
The jovial giants live each day.

Rumbles in the Celestial Circus

Underneath the starry dome,
A circus of delight is home.
With ringmasters and jugglers bold,
Giant fun, a sight to behold.

The clowns trip over cosmic beams,
Spilling poppy seeds and cream-filled dreams.
The audience roars as they collide,
In a whirl of jest, they can't abide.

Trapeze acts swing from star to star,
Twisting and swirling, oh, how bizarre!
With silly pranks and laughter bright,
They fill the cosmos with pure delight.

As the show ends, they dance with flare,
Leaving giggles hanging in the air.
Across the sky, their echoes play,
In this circus where they'll always stay.

Ballooning Beyond the Horizon

Up and away in balloons so round,
The giants float without a sound.
With giggles caught on winds so free,
They drift and soar, as light as can be.

From pastel shores to cotton peaks,
Their laughter whispers, joy it seeks.
With every bounce upon the breeze,
They tickle clouds, oh what a tease!

They chase the sun, their faces bright,
Through skies of blue, in pure delight.
Ballooning high with hearts so light,
A wondrous sight from morn till night.

In colors bold, they paint the air,
Leaving trails of joy everywhere.
Adventure waits where dreams align,
With every laugh, their spirits shine.

Farting Friends of the Firmament

In the skies where laughter flows,
Friends of powdery fluff, who knows?
With silly sounds that echo wide,
They burst out laughing, never hide.

Each little toot sends ripples far,
Creating giggles like a star.
They dance in unison, loud and proud,
With every puff, they form a cloud.

They play their pranks on moonlit nights,
With rumbling joy, like playful fights.
Tooting tunes that mix with cheer,
Their raucous laughter fills the sphere.

As dawn arrives, they bid goodbye,
Leaving echoes in the sky.
Farting friends of the fun-filled glee,
In every heart, they'll always be.

Floating Follies in the Blue

In a realm where the clouds go zoom,
A bouncy bubble fills up the room.
Laughter drifts on the cottony waves,
As silly shapes frolic and misbehave.

Puffy critters in a bright balloon,
Twirling and flipping beneath the moon.
They chase each other in zany flights,
Painting the sky with giggly delights.

With every twist, a chuckle escapes,
As the fluffykins dance in swirly capes.
They tumble and roll, a wobbly crew,
Creating a ruckus, it's quite the view.

In this lighthearted aerial spree,
Where joy and whimsy flow wild and free.
Every hiccup a burst of delight,
Bubbles of laughter pierce the sky bright.

Chortles from Cirrus Sanctuaries

Above the world where the breezes play,
Cloud critters gather for the funny display.
With fuzzy hats and oversized shoes,
They jiggle and jive with outrageous hues.

A fluffy elephant dances on air,
Next to a cat with a curly black hair.
Each giggle sends ripples through the blue,
As they plan silly stunts none can construe.

They swing on the tails of raindrop streams,
Crafting giggles from the light of their dreams.
While shadows play peek a boo on the ground,
Bubbles of humor are swirling around.

In this haven where laughter is born,
Every grumble turns into a horn.
As they float on whispers, the joy unfurls,
A carnival of chuckles in a world of swirls.

Sky-Surfing Silliness

On surfboards made of cotton candy white,
The cloud riders glide, what a dizzying sight!
With waves of giggles, they splash and dive,
Spinning and twirling in a frothy jive.

A penguin in shades rides a fluffy crest,
While dolphins pull pranks, oh what a jest!
The seagulls cackle, joining the fun,
Under a sun that shines like a bun.

Gusts of laughter on breezy tubes,
As friends unite in hilarious grooves.
The stars peek down with a twinkling cheer,
While clouds shift shapes with a comedic leer.

Every swoop and every wild spin,
Brings forth chuckles, a jubilant din.
In this circus floating high above,
The joy rides the wind like a feathered dove.

Witty Whirlwinds

Whirlwinds twirl with a giggly swirl,
As they take a spin, watch chaos unfurl.
With hats and canes, they dance in the sky,
A merry band of jesters flying high.

Each gust of chuckles blows through the air,
Tickling noses and tousling hair.
They scoop up laughter in all their whirl,
Creating mischief with every twirl.

A whirlwind spins in a playful loop,
Chasing dandelions that giggle and droop.
Around they go in a frolicsome race,
They grin and chuckle, a light-hearted space.

With every whoosh, a burst of delight,
As creatures join in, a silly sight.
In this raucous dance with the wind's embrace,
Joy bounces freely in a whimsical chase.

Airborne Giggles

In a sky so blue and bright,
Clouds dance and swirl in delight.
With puffs and poofs, they play all day,
Tickling the sun's warm rays.

Laughter echoes in the breeze,
As fluffy forms stretch with ease.
They leap and bound, a comical sight,
Filling our hearts with pure delight.

A whoosh, a whiff, a funny sound,
Cotton candy fluffs abound.
With every gust, a squeal or two,
Joy spills out, bright and true.

Up above, where fun is free,
Whispers float with giggles glee.
Nature's jesters, light and spry,
Inviting us to laugh and fly.

Playful Puffs above the Earth

Puffy clouds in playful dance,
Whirl and twirl, they take a chance.
With every gust, they bounce and sway,
Creating joy throughout the day.

Tiny breezes tease the trees,
Causing laughter in the leaves.
As shadows slide on sunny ground,
Giggles echo all around.

Whispers linger in the air,
Cheeky breezes everywhere.
A frolicsome breeze, a ticklish air,
Bringing smiles and lightness there.

Dancing droplets, gleeful spritz,
Crackling laughter, fun in fits.
Floating high, they'll steal your grin,
With every burst, the fun begins!

Joyful Jests of the Atmosphere

Up above, the jesters play,
With mischief brightening the day.
Wobbly shapes bring smiles anew,
Painting the sky in hues so blue.

Puffs of air, a sneaky tease,
Carry laughter with the breeze.
A tickle here, a nudge so light,
Chasing shadows, pure delight.

Giggling clouds in their parade,
Tricks and pranks that never fade.
Each squishy float, a bubbly cheer,
Lifting spirits, far and near.

In this realm, where laughter reigns,
Bubbles burst with joyful gains.
So let's embrace the silly, bright,
With every chuckle, life feels light!

Thunderous Chuckles

In stormy skies, a rumble beer,
A hearty laugh, we sense it here.
With every clap, the giggles grow,
As carefree spirits instinctively flow.

Crackling laughter fills the air,
Beneath those clouds, we have no care.
Join the thunder, join the fun,
Let's dance and spin till day is done.

When raindrops fall, they splash like jokes,
Each droplet sings, each puddle pokes.
Nature's humor, loud and clear,
Invites us all to hold it dear.

With every storm, a chuckle loud,
Unity slips in like a cloud.
So raise your voice, don't keep it straight,
Join the laughter, it's never too late!

Riddle of the Roaring Winds

In a land where breezes sing,
Laughter dances, tickles spring.
Puffy clouds roll, bright and round,
Whispers of humor in every sound.

A great big gust, a whoosh of fun,
Chasing giggles, on the run.
With every puff, a chuckle shared,
In this breeze, no one is spared.

What brings the smiles from ear to ear?
A whirlwind of joy, come gather near.
Silly sounds, like a trumpet's blare,
As the winds weave tales beyond compare.

Mirthful puffs at break of day,
Chasing worries far away.
With each round breeze, a hearty cheer,
Join the riddle, let laughter steer.

Caverns of Cheerful Gales

Deep in caverns where breezes play,
Joyful echoes brighten the gray.
Bouncing off walls, a chorus sings,
Life's too short, enjoy the swings.

A ticklish draft, oh what a tease,
Twirling hats and swaying trees.
Every gust a playful jest,
Cheerful whispers, they never rest.

In shadowed caves, where shadows prance,
Even stones join in the dance.
Laughter rolls like a thunder clap,
In these caverns, take a lap.

So step inside, let laughter flow,
In cheerful gales, let your spirit glow.
Every chuckle, every jest,
Here in the cave, we're truly blessed.

Floating Freckles of Joy

In the sky, where bright spots race,
Freckles of joy, in playful space.
Bouncing beams of laughter light,
A sprinkle of fun, a wild delight.

Bubbles float on a sunny beam,
Carrying whispers of a silly dream.
As they pop, they burst with cheer,
Spreading giggles to far and near.

Like starlit laughs that twinkle and fly,
Freckles of mirth scatter the sky.
Catch them quick, the fleeting smiles,
Chase them onward, across the miles.

With every giggle, a story blooms,
Floating bliss in joyous rooms.
Let the freckles of laughter grow,
As we soar high, let our spirits glow.

Giggles in the Upper Stratosphere

Up above, where the bright winds gleam,
Giggles linger, like a dream.
Clouds act silly, shadows play,
Laughter echoes, come what may.

In the stratosphere, where seraphs laugh,
Joy spills out from the gentle draft.
Tickled pink by the playful breeze,
Everyone joins in with silly ease.

Whirling, twirling, in blissful flight,
What a sight, a pure delight!
Sounding like chimes in the starry night,
Here among clouds, everything feels right.

So laugh aloud, let worries flee,
In the upper realm, where hearts feel free.
Giggles abound, they never cease,
In our sky-high playground, find your peace.

Whispers of Floating Behemoths

In the sky so high and wide,
Big creatures drift, they take a ride.
With a puff and a playful gruff,
They spread joy, it's all in the fluff.

Chasing clouds, a breezy dance,
Every wobble, a chance romance.
With rumbles low, and giggles loud,
They frolic here, a fluffy crowd.

Tickles and tugs, a silliness surge,
In the air, they laugh and merge.
Whispers float on gentle winds,
A world where silly never ends.

So look above, join in the fun,
With every puff, laughter's begun.
These gentle giants, full of cheer,
In every giggle, magic's near.

Laughter Among the Clouds

High above, where the giggles soar,
Joyful beings drift and explore.
With a hitch and a bubbly puff,
They play on waves, full of fluff.

Jolly jests in the airy sweep,
Their chuckles wake the world from sleep.
Softly swirling in a game,
Dancing clouds, never the same.

They tickle the sun, a radiant beam,
A chorus of laughter, a whimsical dream.
With plumes that sway and twirls that tease,
Life up here is a playful breeze.

Each twinkling star can't help but smile,
As giggles echo mile by mile.
Between the puffs and rolling light,
A world of laughter shines so bright.

The Melody of Rumbles

Bellowing from up above, so grand,
A melody floats through the land.
With every rumble, a playful note,
They paint the sky in laughter's coat.

While the sun dips low, tunes fill the air,
Soft giggles dance without a care.
Each bubble of sound, pure delight,
A symphony sparkles, oh so bright.

Watch them jive in hazy hues,
A chuckling chorus, never to snooze.
With breezes that hum and twirl around,
The echoes of giggles resound.

In this orchestra, joy takes flight,
Under love's canvas, pure and white.
A rumble, a laugh, a skywide cheer,
In every sound, happiness is here.

Cosmic Cackles Under the Stars

Beneath a sky of twinkling beams,
A wondrous sight of playful dreams.
Where laughter sprinkles like a star,
Cosmic beings wander far.

With each burst of light, a giggle grows,
In the cosmic dance, joy overflows.
Soft chuckles ride the night's cool breath,
A symphony of life, beyond all death.

Starlit whispers, a tale unfolds,
Of friendly giants, brave and bold.
With shimmering laughs that fill the air,
They make the universe a joyous affair.

So gaze above, let the laughter roll,
In the vastness, find your soul.
For among the stars, delight takes wing,
In the night's embrace, let your heart sing.

Tumultuous Tumbles among the Stars

Floating high in skies so wide,
Wobbling worlds take each wild ride.
Twinkling stars start to laugh and play,
As they swirl in the milky way.

Cosmic leaps with bouncy flair,
Joyful orbs dance without a care.
Meteor showers bring squeaky sounds,
As giggles echo around in bounds.

Planets party, spinning bright,
Silly comets zoom with delight.
All creation joins in the fun,
Underneath the cosmic sun.

In this chaos, wonder flows,
As laughter through the heavens grows.
Each tumble brings more joy and cheers,
With twinkling lights that glimmer near.

Stormy Smiles

Clouds roll in with a grin so wide,
Whirling winds that don't want to hide.
Thunder rumbles with a hearty chuckle,
While raindrops bounce like a playful shuffle.

Lightning flashes, a jester's show,
Each crack a giggle, a quickened glow.
Puddles splash with joyful shouts,
As nature dances, without doubts.

Winds weave tales of merry mirth,
While stormy skies hold whimsical birth.
They twist and turn, a lively spree,
Creating a symphony, wild and free.

In the frolic of the tempest's play,
Every storm brings laughter our way.
Winds whisper secrets, soft and sweet,
As the world beneath skips to the beat.

Clouds that Chuckle

Puffy wisps float, giggling high,
Painting the canvas of the sky.
Tickled by breezes, they sway and spin,
In a fluffy world where grins begin.

They morph and twist, a silly sight,
Crafting shapes that bring delight.
A rabbit here, a dragon there,
Each form dissolves without a care.

As sunshine beams down, they burst with glee,
Dancing lightly, wild and free.
When raindrops fall, it's just a tease,
Each one a joke riding the breeze.

In the sky, where happiness flows,
The perfect place for chuckles to grow.
Floating freely, they play their roles,
Tickling hearts and warming souls.

Boisterous Breezes

Whirling winds weave through the trees,
Carrying whispers, secrets, and tease.
Playful gusts chase leaves around,
With a merry dance, joy is found.

Ticklish breezes with a playful shout,
Tickle your cheeks, spin you about.
They rustle grass, create a song,
In this playful romp, nothing's wrong.

With every swirl, a chuckle flies,
As the fluffy clouds race by.
Nature's laughter fills the air,
As breezes toss and sway without a care.

In breezy antics, fun's abloom,
Chasing smiles and banishing gloom.
Nature's jesters, frolicking free,
Singing together, wild as can be.

Raucous Roars of Laughter

In the sky, a puffball strayed,
With a snicker and a cheeky spade.
Round and round, in a silly dance,
Blowing bubbles, given half a chance.

A cloud with a wig, oh what a sight,
Tickling the sun with sheer delight.
Down below, kids laugh and play,
Chasing giggles that float away.

Whispers of chuckles in the breeze,
Frolicking friends among the trees.
Every pop and fizz, a joyful cheer,
Filling the air with loud good cheer.

With each wild burst of shiny air,
Laughter erupts, in joy we share.
A raucous season of smiles so wide,
As happiness bounces from side to side.

Stratospheric Shenanigans

Floating up high, a balloon with glee,
Wobbling and wobbling, oh so free.
Its colors swirl in the bright sunlight,
Chasing rainbows, an aerial flight.

Giggles erupt from a distant cloud,
Puffing up hearts, making us proud.
With every bounce, a joke they tell,
Riding the winds, casting a spell.

Laughter sparked from pockets of air,
As our spirits swirl without a care.
Dizzying whirlwinds of mirth translate,
Into sunshine and joy—how great!

The sky's a playground of whimsical sights,
With playful spirits buzzing like kites.
So let your giggles soar and ascend,
In this frolic, let the fun never end!

Delightful Draughts of Joy

A frothy brew spills from the sky,
With pops and fizzles, oh my, oh my!
Each sip is filled with a chuckling sound,
As bubbles float gently around.

Chubby cheeks with smiles so wide,
Chasing the bubbles that bounce and slide.
What a treat, to share this bliss,
As laughter dances, can't help but miss!

Sipping delights as the sun shines bright,
Mixing happiness, pure delight.
Joy overflows, in a sprightly stream,
While giggles gust forth—a playful dream.

Every droplet, a tickle, a cheer,
As we sip on avowals of good cheer.
With every taste, another giggle ignites,
In this world of laughter, everything feels right.

Mirthful Monsters of the Sky

Grinning faces in the clouds above,
Wobbling forms we can't help but love.
They shake and shimmy, causing a scene,
With belly laughs and a joyous sheen.

Chasing the moon with a raucous roar,
These playful beings we simply adore.
Floating high, they sprinkle delight,
With each silly jig, they set hearts alight.

A whirlwind of joy spins 'round and 'round,
In soft cotton fluff where magic is found.
Their giggles bubble and bounce through the air,
Sharing their laughter, a gift so rare.

Let's join in the frolic, share in the fun,
With each goofy grin, our hearts become one.
In this lively jest, let spirits fly,
In the realm of the joyful, reaching the sky!

Breezy Behemoth Serenade

In the clouds, they dance so bright,
Twirling joy, a comic sight.
With snores that rattle the blue dome,
They giggle loud, far from home.

Wobbling around with cheerful flair,
They send soft breezes through the air.
A laugh escapes, a thunderous roar,
And all the skies begin to soar.

Each step a bounce, a playful leap,
Their laughter echoes, never deep.
Beneath the sun, they frolic and play,
Turning the mundane into a holiday.

With every gust, their spirits soar,
Chasing rainbows, they always want more.
A jolly tune, a gentle cheer,
In this grand big sky, joy is near.

Jovial Titans of the Sky

Boys and girls, look up high,
See the titans pass by.
With every puff, they shake the ground,
Laughter echoes all around.

From fluffy heads to bouncing feet,
They jiggle and wiggle to the beat.
With each explosion of silly sound,
Clouds start bouncing all around.

Their giant forms twist and sway,
Making mischief every day.
Cracking jokes as they float by,
Painting giggles across the sky.

With a wink and a whimsical smile,
They'd dance and frolic for a while.
In their embrace, let worries cease,
For they bring moments of pure peace.

Nebulae of Chuckles

In the velvet void, they twirl and spin,
With every huff, their joy begins.
Bright ribbons swirl, colors collide,
In a cosmic dance, they take pride.

Weightless laughter fills the dark,
As stars join in to leave a mark.
Their antics splash the night with fun,
Sprinkling joy 'til the night is done.

Giggles burst from stellar bloom,
Lighting up the vastest room.
With every twinkling chuckle shared,
They craft a universe, joy declared.

Floating further, beyond the veil,
No frown can stay in their trail.
So raise your voice and sing along,
For laughter is where we all belong.

The Great Puffball Parade

Gather around, it's time to cheer,
For the fluffy brigade is finally here!
With buoyant steps, they march with glee,
A whimsical sight for all to see.

Jubilant puffs of every hue,
Bouncing happily, they follow through.
With every gust, they twist and sway,
Creating a splendor, bright and gay.

They blow up balloons filled with laughs,
Releasing joy through funny gaffes.
Each cloud a smile in the bright display,
In their frolics, gloom slips away.

Watch their antics, a delightful spree,
They paint the world like a jubilee.
So join the march, let giggles ignite,
In this parade of pure delight!

Celestial Chuckles

In the sky where colors play,
The big ones dance and sway.
With a puff, they send a breeze,
Tickling leaves on all the trees.

Bubbles float and softly pop,
As the laughter reaches top.
Stars giggle with a twinkling gleam,
In a world where fun's a dream.

Clouds chase one another 'round,
Making gentle, silly sounds.
A game of hide-and-seek they bring,
Joyful echoes on the wing.

With each twist and turn they boast,
Creating laughter, laughter most!
Filling the night with cheerful sights,
Underneath the starry lights.

The Breezy Giants' Capers

Up above in skies so wide,
The hefty ones take a ride.
With a chuckle and a laugh,
They tug at tails of comets' path.

Rolling round in fluffy beds,
They tease with breezy, swirling threads.
Whispers blow through trees so tall,
As they play and prance and sprawl.

The moon winks down at all the fun,
While sunlight glimmers, day begun.
Each puff transforms, a dance anew,
Under a canopy of blue.

From distant shores, the echoes rise,
Joining in with squeals and sighs.
These hefty friends are quite a sight,
In realms where joy shines so bright.

Drifting Through a Symphony of Laughter

Floating softly on the breeze,
They share their joy with wiggly leaves.
A symphony of chuckles grand,
As sunny rays lend them a hand.

With every twist, a new surprise,
Sounds of laughter reach the skies.
A cacophony of playful glee,
Encircles all in harmony.

With fluff and poof, they dance around,
Creating ripples in the sound.
Each airy leap is filled with cheer,
While merry tunes float far and near.

Suspended between earth and star,
The frolics echo near and far.
A symphony that never ends,
In a world where joy transcends.

Echoes of Expansive Echoes

In an expanse where laughter flies,
Resonating through the skies.
A chorus of chuckles, round and bright,
Flowing freely in the night.

With playful whispers, winds do tease,
Carrying tales among the trees.
Their vastness holds a merry tune,
Bouncing high like a bright balloon.

Clouds puff up like cotton candy,
With joys that feel so ever handy.
Each echo tells a story bold,
Of wonders new and joys untold.

In this realm of frolic and flight,
Every giggle feels so right.
A canvas painted with delight,
Where expansive echoes fill the night.

Frivolous Fluctuations

A wobbly dance, round and round,
Chubby forms bounce off the ground.
Tickles of laughter fill the air,
As jolly friends tumble without a care.

Round puffy cheeks and silly grins,
Bouncing about like playful twins.
Each puff a giggle, each leap a sigh,
In the wispy clouds, we soar up high.

Gyrating softly like clouds so airy,
Every twist and turn, quite contrary.
Amidst the silliness, the fun erupts,
As chuckles and giggles are happily cupped.

So let the wind carry our cheer,
As we play and laugh without any fear.
In the lovely sights of blissful flight,
We'll dance with joy until the night.

The Great Ballooning Frolic

Inflated dreams drift through the sky,
Floating high, oh my, oh my!
Wobbly wonders in bright array,
As blimps of laughter sway and play.

With squeaks and honks like trumpets loud,
We bounce on air, both silly and proud.
Round fluffy forms with bouncy grace,
In a whirl of fun, we pick up pace.

Each gentle sway brings a joyful squeal,
As airships dance with a giddy feel.
In hues of color, they pirouette,
Creating gales of joy we won't forget.

High above trees, the antics unfold,
With every twist, more stories told.
So let's embrace this buoyant spree,
As laughter fills the air, wild and free.

Airborne Antics and Jests

Bouncing and bobbing in puffy attire,
Chasing the clouds, hearts filled with fire.
With a whoosh and a swirl, we twist around,
In the circus of skies, fun can be found.

Silly charms in a zany ballet,
Twirling in rhythm, come join the play.
Every giggle floats like a feather,
Together we trample the weight of the weather.

Laughter erupts like bubbles in space,
In joyful chaos, we find our place.
Through wind and whimsy, our spirits soar,
Each happy stumble, we share even more.

As balloons drift, we leap and sway,
In bursts of laughter, we frolic and play.
Let joy be the tether, the essence for all,
For who doesn't rise when the giggles call?

Heavenly Hilarity

In the realm where whimsies gleam,
Wacky tales burst in vibrant dreams.
We float like bubbles, light as air,
Wide-eyed wonders, without a care.

Guffaws float high as bright stars twinkle,
Dancing shadows, who seek to sprinkle.
On laughter's breeze we ride the tide,
In a joyous journey we won't divide.

Every step we take creates a jig,
Silly sounds, both sweet and big.
Surprises hidden in every twist,
In the playful storm, you can't resist.

Under the vault of laughter's sky,
Join the parade, let your spirit fly.
With a puff of cheer and chuckles galore,
In the land of fun, who could ask for more?

www.ingramcontent.com/pod-product-compliance
Lightning Source LLC
Chambersburg PA
CBHW072148200426
43209CB00051B/840